BLACK HOLES WITHIN US

Marta Markoska

Proverse Hong Kong

2021

In her metaphysical poetry collection, *Black Holes Within Us*, Marta Markoska calls the universe into play, as both the context for her love and as providing a means for its expression. Her poems of love are full of ordinary details from everyday modern living, but are paradoxically pervaded with classical, philosophical and scientific allusions. They contain interesting and perceptive ideas – for example, about the self, the continuous skirmishes between the sexes on topics as various as the day's meals and sexual fulfilment – expressed in simple words and images, and are, at different levels, accessible to all.

Macedonian writer, Marta Markoska, was born in Skopje, R. Macedonia, in 1981. She has a background in General and Comparative Literature and Cultural Studies, and is published in these areas. She is also known as an award-winning poet and short story winning writer. Markoska is also well-known to audiences from her project, *Marta's Palace*, and from "The Campaign to show the Beauty of a Woman After Breast Cancer", which she launched at the same time as the first monolingual English-language edition of her *H/ERO/T/IC BOOK*, also published by Proverse Hong Kong.

BLACK HOLES

WITHIN US

Marta Markoska

Translated by
Aleksandra Spaseska

BLACK HOLES WITHIN US
By Marta Markoska
First monolingual English-language edition
published in Hong Kong by Proverse Hong Kong,
under exclusive licence, September 2021.

ISBN 13:978-988-8492-32-9 / 9789888492329 (Paperback);
ISBN 13: 978-988-8492-33-6 / 9789888492336 (Ebook).

Enquiries to Proverse Hong Kong
P.O. Box 259, Tung Chung Post Office,
Lantau, NT, Hong Kong SAR, China.
Email: proverse@netvigator.com;
Web: www.proversepublishing.com

Cover design by Artist Hong Kong.

British Library Cataloguing in Publication Data
A catalogue record for the first paperback edition
is available from the British Library

PUBLISHERS' INTRODUCTION

We first met the poet Marta Markoska in August 2014 in Romania, when she and we were invited participants at the annual event, The International Festival Curtea D'Argeş Poetry Nights, organised by Carolina Ilica and Dumitru M. Ion. As others did, we exchanged copies of our poetic monographs and we were very impressed by BLACK HOLES WITHIN US, the volume she gifted to us. It goes without saying that we are very pleased that Marta has entrusted us as her publishers for the first monolingual English-language edition of this work.

At the time we met, we did not know what Marta was facing, but later we learnt that she was then extremely ill and was even unsure if she would survive. The bilingual, Macedonian-English first edition of her H/ERO/T/IC BOOK (2019) is a product of her situation. Later, in 'The story behind H/ERO/T/IC BOOK', her introduction to the first monolingual English-language edition of this work, published a year later, she describes her experiences and the steps she took, after the operation, to change her outlook, personality and physique. The transformation has been extraordinary! We encourage readers to obtain Marta Markoska's, H/ERO/T/IC BOOK, and read 'The story behind H/ERO/T/IC BOOK' in its entirety for themselves.

We first spoke with Marta Markoska in a shoe shop in Curtea D'Argeş, on the way to a programmed festival event. Marta was considering a pair of shoes and we left the shop while she was still deciding. Later, she told us that she had come to the conclusion that she could do without them. The bilingual Macedonian-English first edition of BLACK HOLES WITHIN US was already published by then. We wonder whether the poem, 'All Loves Are Like Shoes', will ever be revised to include a decision like this?

BLACK HOLES WITHIN US
Marta Markoska

“***We should leave the truth to the Gods***”

LIFE IS A CYCLE

(CIRCUS)

LIFE IS LIKE A BAZAAR

We buy the moments of happiness,
unaware that underneath the surface of its fruits
all that's left are the rotten legumes,
filling up the content of life's little bag
only to gain weight!

LIFE IS LIKE TEA

Taking your time deciding how you desire it,
Not being able to decide even between two kinds;
It takes minutes to reach boiling point,
but much longer to cool down so you can taste it:
You consume it to the last drop and feel thirsty anew.

LIFE IS LIKE SIPPING COFFEE WHILE YOU READ A QUATRAIN

Anxiously rushing to taste it before it gets cold,
Sipping so it would last a little longer;
Immediately you are ready for more;
but, the coffee sediment in the cup testifies to another consummated delight…

LIFE IS LIKE A GAME OF SQUASH

Imagine the world as a game of squash
and all the people as players in the field.
That way it's easier to accept
that all the moves do not depend on you alone,
nor can you give your best game.
The result does not depend on your skills, nor can you expect
a sure win.
You simply play without desire of knowing the end,
Play with no desire to defeat the opponent;
For your moves are conditioned
by the moves of the other players;
and the skillful swing at the ball
depends on how it's thrown at you.

Therefore – winning the game is utterly irrelevant,
playing it is a privilege of the living!

CATACHRESIS OF THE SPIRIT

(UNDER)STUDIES OF LIFE

I tried to save you from vain thoughts,
Telling you that all in this world is an illusion
and we are just slaves of our own ideologies;
But, mure to the point, it was the jolly singer
who managed with lightness, time and again,
to shake the fat layers from the lives of strangers.

You only live once
This life is too short

No, I am not a spiritual teacher, I tell you,
I don't know the Vedas and the Upanishads,
I don't know the Shastras and the Sutras,
I don't know the Kabbalah and The Holy Book,
I don't know the Torah and the Quran.

I do know that in this world
We are the Shudras,
We are the Kurban.

TEA(RFUL) COOKIES

to Goran

when in my cup of tea I dip
an O-shaped cookie, I think of you,
although your name starts with a different letter...
And when I suck in that juicy plumped cookie,
I think of you saying:
– don't buy these tea(rful) cookies,
because when I drink tea, you drink coffee. Are we supposed to be tearful,
since we both cannot enjoy
the taste of these tea cookies?

And I thought of saying, although I didn't,
– Remember not the taste of the cookie,
but the time spent passionately enjoying it...
At least you should conserve these precious moments,
for I am not Proust, and even he didn't solve
the issue of time lost.

ENLIGHTEN(MENT)

Your vocabulary is smaller than my library;
Your fantasies are fewer than my drinks at the bar:
But your vices outnumber my books and my drinks.
And yet you are considered a saint,
for you never start the day without a "line" (*nulla dies sine linea*).

(F)AIRED ATTITUDES

You've aged
When food becomes your best friend
and most frequent guest,
when erotic movies make you yawn
and horror ones put you to sleep,
when lunch excites you more
than seeing your husband;
when not even a quote by Alan Ford makes you laugh;
nor a scene by Woody Allen,
nor a Jay Leno show;
when you listen to the music of the 80s,
claiming that nothing good has been produced since,
when you read the classics over and over again
but have no idea who won last year's Nobel Prize,
when you smell of *Pino Silvestre*
and your partner asks if it's *Hugo Boss*,
when people your age compliment your looks
but the camera alone convinces you
that they are wrong!

(UN)CONSCIOUSNESS

We used to spend hours talking:
Now we spend hours – in silence!

PEARLS OF WISDOM (NONE THE WISER)

You are lonely,
I am lonely;
All women are overrated,
All men are chauvinists;
All women are conceited,
All men are frustrated;
All women are spoiled,
All men are choosy;
All women are adulteresses,
All men are egoists.

While we call each other names,
Scolding each other,
Blaming each other,
Cursing each other with
Merits and labels,
There is a whole world of single
but desperate and miserable men and women,
just as there are heaps of food
and so many people starving!

HERETIC/EROTIC PHILOSOPHY

No, you're no Proust,
You are just a prude!

You don't know my cyrillic alphabet
and I don't understand your writings
scribbled in a German notebook
with a Swiss pen
and thoughts – eclectic

Standing beside one another
like the latest Volvo
and an ox in a Volvo
like North and South Korea
like Oedipus and the Sphinx...

Don't waste your days on me...
My Chinese bag is not worthy
of your Japanese laptop
My southern sensuality is not worthy
of your western rationalism

We would have had a future
had we lived in the past!

(CU)RATING LIFE

When I was only fifteen,
I longed for you to hold me for hours.
Now you hold me for hours
and I long to be fifteen again.

(PO)ET(H)ICS OF SUFFERING

Life is like a pimple:
you need to press it right,
squeeze all the toxic and harmful
fluids out of it...
Only after it bleeds
and there is nothing left inside,
will you be able to start over,
hoping it won't scar...

Although you're replacing one ugliness with another,
The scar is the only way
to put an end to what makes you ugly
– on the inside!

(C)OM(M)IT(MENT) FOREVER

Till death do us part!
... what they failed to notice was
what tore them apart was – life!

END(S) OF THE WORLD

The North is at war with the South,
The East with the West:
Even if we were a herd
we would've understood
the West contains
– Unrest!
The North holds the Forth
And the South – the Drought;

Measuring our tolerance
in segments,
while the circle defies
the square, and you defy me,
nagging,
what shall we eat today!

AREAS OF LOVE

YOU ARE FULL OF STORIES AND HERE I AM WRITING YOU POEMS!

You speak seven languages,
I am barely cooing in one;
You conquered Everest and Kilimanjaro,
And I get dizzy riding the Panorama in the park;
You walk three kilometers a day,
I can't even make it to the neighbour's;
You are able to see which lights are on the Vodno Cross,*
And I need glasses to sort out the rice;
You gulp wine while quoting Homer,
And I get drunk with a kind word;
You pick wild roses with bare hands,
And I pretend to be Little Briar Rose so that you'd kiss me;
You toured Europe on a bike;
And I followed you on Facebook sitting cross-legged.

And so it goes...

While you were swimming a marathon,
I was singing in the shower;
While you hurried to get to me;
I gave you up in my dreams

Because you are full of stories,
And I write you poems!

*The Vodno Cross, known as the Millennium Cross, is a 66-metre tall cross situated on the top of Vodno Mountain in the Republic of North Macedonia above the capital city of Skopje. Built in 2002, it is one of the tallest crosses in the world.

THE ESSENCE OF LOVE

You measure my restlessness
with the pimples on your chin;

You measure my passion
with the length of your sideburns;

You measure my virtue
with the depth of my earlobes;

You measure my love
by the distance between my eyes;

You measure my youth
with the pills that keep you healthy;

You measure my soul
with the length of your forearms;

You measure my essence
with the electricity and heating bills.
* * *
I like writing numbers between
the chin,
the sideburns,
the earlobes,
your eyes,
the forearms....

I like telling you
that you are not the only one
taking pills to satisfy my youth;

Nor the only one
who pays the electricity and heating bills!

LOGIC OF THE STRONGER ONE

A medusa left in a dry place,
does not prove that the sea
has lost its function!

LOGIC OF THE WEAKER ONE

If all people are mortal
And all truth relative
And if all deities are imaginary
And you are my deity...

Am I allowed to conclude that
You are just an imaginary deity
which performed its function relatively well,
while I was dying to prove that
you really existed and performed miracles?

APPLIED KNOWLEDGE

APPLIED HISTORY

If you knew a little bit more history,
you would've understood that I didn't need
the Saemiramide Gardens,
Nor the Tower of Babel;
All I ever needed were conquerors,
who would bestow importance on my fortress...

But not for the sake of building empires together,
and not for the sake of reigning together;
for all empires collapse from within
and any joint governance
leads to mutual rivalry...

All I needed was your warfare skills
to teach me how to fight my own vanity,
so I can overcome – myself!

APPLIED GEOGRAPHY

If you don't make the effort to cross
nine hills,
nine fields,
nine seas,
to get to my shores...
then I won't let you sail
down to my enclave,
where an island of hidden treasures awaits you
and the only thing missing is your ivory.

APPLIED BIOLOGY

If the nucleus of our problems lies
in the different interpretation of invertebrates,
and if your amoebic nature
does not allow me to establish your character,
that means that the Leo in your horoscope
is just a lurking hyena!

APPLIED CHEMISTRY

If you claim that I am your oxygen,
you'd better hope you are not my hydrogen,
because then this relationship would be ... stagnant water!

APPLIED MATHEMATICS

If you can calculate
the square root of your stupidity,
and subtract from that the square root of my patience,
then multiply that by the will to forgive,
and add to it every new beginning,
– you will understand that our equation
is divisible by ZERO!

APPLIED PHYSICS

You said,
If I throw you off the balcony
and then jump after you,
I will fall first
because of the mass force,
although we have the same momentum.

But, if I only throw you
and I change my mind,
Then the law of free falling
is a small comfort to Ethics as a science!

APPLIED ASTRONOMY

While you're telling me
nothing has changed,
the cosmos has spread and
we are now galaxies
further away from each other!

While you're telling me
that it's cloudy inside your soul
and my aura is sun-filled,
I remind you that the theory of chaos
is rooted in meteorology.

While you're telling me
that we should have stopped time
when love had greatest density
and our bodies greatest magnetic force,
I remind you that the black holes
were made of self-implosions
and now they exist inside of us!

APPLIED SOCIOLOGY

Humanity overcame
fascism and antisemitism,
nuclear disasters,
natural cataclysms;

And you can't get over
the fact that I am keeping my last name,
and that I don't know how to make bread rolls
or cabbage and leek pie.

Yet our triumph is inevitable,
not because of the understanding,
not because of the tolerance,
not because of the forgiveness,
not because of the respect;

Our triumph is inevitable,
due to the discovery that
imbalance is a natural state,
and order is a side effect to chaos;

Our triumph is inevitable,
due to the discoveries of imbalanced physics;
due to the acceptance of the principle of indetermination; due
to the realization of the sensitivity of the primary condition!

APPLIED DEFENSE SCIENCE

After I kicked you out like a pawn from a chess table,
while you persistently tried to guard me like a queen,
you should have known that the rooks and knights
are only part of the game,
and can never harm the queen,
surrounded by real pawns,
even when the king is out of the game.

APPLIED ASTROLOGY

You are like a daily horoscope;
I read it, then immediately erase it.

APPLIED ECONOMICS

I spent you even before I earned you,
with your interest rate far exceeding
my ability to pay you back.
Now we are doomed to live
as debtors to pleasures,
paying off our loaned love
for two lifetimes!

APPLIED RELATIVITY

You ask me
why can't you satisfy me as I can satisfy you;
I tell you
that the two-dimensional geometry of your plane
can not be applied to my sphere.

HOLOGRAM OF HAPPINESS

CONSTIPATED

Tears are like faeces...
Like the excrement that, if kept
and denied an exit,
will constipate you...

Same with the tears you won't let go
whenever they need to run...
they'll constipate your soul!

ALL LOVES ARE LIKE SHOES

All loves are like shoes:

Those we carefully treasure
and wear only on special occasions;
ultimately unused and outgrown, they've shrunk;
yet their beauty is still preserved
but now useless;
and we reprimand ourselves that
we didn't enjoy them more often.

Those we wear every day
with such great pleasure,
enjoying them over and over again,
are the first to wear out and fade,
as we spend them and toss them out,
regretting we didn't buy
two pairs of the same,
so that they would last longer,
so that we have a reserve,
so that we may rejoice at the idea
that we can wear them
whenever we want to.

The ones that endure the most
are the ones we actually like the least,
so we push them aside;
we misplace them in the back of the closet;
we ignore them for weeks, months, years,
only to realize after a long time
that they were always there for us,
although we forgot and ignored them,
and have never worn them with joy!

SYNCOPATED ARRHYTHMIA

I won't let them deaden my will and build cemeteries on it –
yet they do

I won't let them mutilate my spirit so they can revel over it –
yet they do

I won't let them hide my rainbow under their black or white
thoughts – yet they do

I won't let them take the smile off my face and draw scars on
it – yet they do

I won't let them take my visions away so they can resurrect
the darkness – yet they do

I won't let them clip my wings so they can stomp over me in
the mud – yet they do

I won't let them confine my imagination so they can live
without illusions – yet they do

I won't let them dose my oxygen so they can breathe with
ease – yet they do

But I will let them take my breath away with their
enlightenment! – if they can ....

Alas, let them do as they wish – I don't feel like writing
poetry anyway!

MISINTERPRETED DREAMS

All directions led to one notion:
the longer you sleep, the less you truly live;
the more you dream, the less vigilant your joy;
And so, misguided by the dream interpretation dictionary,
Instead of "Hollywood" – I ended up at Mount Athos!

COLD TRUTH

We wallow in the despair of our memories,
offering them to others like a freshly white-coated picture,
so they can fill in their memories thinking that:
only their loving is real,
only their problems – misunderstood,
only their lives – meaningless,
only their souls – emptied,
only their knowledge – greatest,
only their fates – predestined,
only their vanities – hurt,
only their memories – immersible,
only their truths – irreversible!

NO ONE IS SAFE FROM ONESELF

You are a human-rights fighter
and I, I only fight for my own....

How could I fight for others,
when, right in front of me, two sparrows
just caught an innocent grasshopper,

And I watched indecisively
whether to help it;

said to myself – it's nature's law.

Had I saved the tiny grasshopper,
I would have starved the sparrows
who might have had offspring:

I took comfort in that. I thought,
perhaps the tiny grasshopper
ate two ants earlier,
who also had their own offspring

I (DON'T) WANT TO

I don't want to wear eyeglasses,
So I won't have to see the desperation in others;
I just want to surmise it...
Drawing wrinkles on their foreheads,
Imagine their lives,
Write new stories about them...

I don't want to wear eyeglasses,
So I don't have to see the fear in others;
I just want to gaze at the sky,
Finish drawing the contours of angels,
Imagine the worlds of the Gods,
Script the destinies of mortals...

AWAKENESS

I woke up from the eternal dream,
where there is no longer spring;
but who can tell what the next lunar phase will bring?

Life awaits, another life in it creeping
where mistakes are repeated unwillingly;
but who can tell if fairytales are told thrillingly?

Perched on their false thrones I see them peeping,
buying kingdoms and putting on crowns;
but who can tell if they are kings or clowns?

BLACK HOLES WITHIN US

ENTROPY OF LOVE

I once made chaos in your system,
not to prove to you the existence of entropy,
generated whenever our two bodies
were in a ratio one to another,
since I said nothing new...
Thermodynamics was invented long ago
and it will remind us for a long time
of the energy lost through interaction…

I once created chaos in your perfect order,
not for the purpose of violating your personal values,
but to comfort you with the fact that such rules of the game
are followed in the cosmos, and we are like two black holes
fused together, sucking energy from one another
harder than was naturally built into the system
and now drained out, hoping to become stars again.

I now assure you that two formations, two bodies, two souls
create much greater entropy
than any individual body for itself!

POEM WITHOUT GRAVITY

I circle around my life
like a free electron,
in a constant orbit searching
and just lurching
and just lurching
and just lurching...

QUANTUM THEORY OF LOVE

We are just like stars
that collapsed
in their own gravity,
and are now weightless,
back to the zero state:
we count time backwards,
so we can claim that it all started with us
and with us it shall end!

COUNTERBALANCE OF REASONING

The Cosmos gravitates towards chaos
And we grovel because of earth's gravity,
so – whether we go up or down –
it is...the same!
Oh Newton I wish you were born in the age of Heisenberg!
...
...
...
Or, if only free falling was weightless!

SALTY-SWEET UNIVERSE

to Igor Isakovski

If we were dreamers on some other planet
and we ate cookies made of nebula,
would we then, as we do now, think about leaving,
or would that have been just as sweet an experience
as my grandmothers' vanilla half-moon cookies?

If we were thinkers on some other planet,
and we ate breadsticks that finish
the straight line of our lives,
would we then, as we do now, think that parallel lines touch
somewhere in infinity,
or would that have been too salty a notion
for people who prefer sweet pleasures?

COMMENTARIES

Elbert Siu Ping Lee

The poetry of Marta Markoska is fundamentally destructive, but beautifully so – like a willful rebel daubing graffiti on city walls. The destructive experience for the rebel is existential, experimental, infused with fear, pleasure and pain. However, what is lost is found, anew – her symbolic destruction of the established opens up for her, and also in a significant way for others, an entirely different universe which no one can ignore.

What is destroyed in Markoska's poetic work is our human centric conceptions of ourselves – values, love, and matters of knowledge and truth showing themselves in different life spheres. She takes them apart and lays them out again, often in terms and terminologies of physics – the discipline that deals with 'dead matter'. The effect of this configuration of words in her poetry is beyond using physical phenomena as metaphors. Instead, it creates a new sense of reality in us – what is so often thought of as uniquely human are in fact immutable laws of physics after all.

In the poem 'Entropy of Love', human love relations are portrayed in terms of thermodynamics, chaos, and entropy. Yes, love that is so endearing to us acts like physical systems attracting, colliding, and interacting to its own final, irreversible destruction:

"I once created chaos in your perfect order
not for the purpose of violating your personal values
but to comfort you with the fact that such rules of the game
are followed in the cosmos, and we are like two black holes
fused together sucking energy from one another..."

Marta's playful destruction of our conceptions of love shows up again In the 'Applied Knowledge' series of poems. What is commonly known as a contest of minds between partners is in fact set and determined by the hard-nosed logic of a mathematical formula – it will not work. The variables that affect love are laid out in an equation in 'Applied Mathematics':

"If you can calculate
the square root of your stupidity
and subtract that from the square root of my patience
…
– you will understand that our equation is divisible by
ZERO!"

Perhaps when love is not seen as love, but as what Markoska suggests; a purely physical phenomenon, as referred to in the poem 'Life is Like a Game of Squash', in which neither parties have complete control, it stops becoming an illusion.

What is left with us then are physical equations and formulae that govern love. But these too are subject to entropy. They say in black holes, no information can be retained. Then perhaps the black holes in us are the only places where the immutable laws of physics are broken. The poetry of Marta Markoska is bleak but enlightening. Each poem forces us to think about matters that are unthinkable – aiming to destroy our favourite beliefs and wishes. What is true, what is good, and what is beautiful to us are, in her poems, almost always certainly not what they seem. Yet, in a strange sort of way, the poet concludes her vision in her opening quote: "We should leave truth to the Gods." Now the urban rebel stands side by side with an unarticulated form of mysticism – we are all just playing here.

—Elbert Siu Ping Lee, author of *Rain on the Pacific Coast*
(Proverse Hong Kong, 2013)
August 2021

Hayley Ann Solomon

Markoska's *Black holes within us* syphons ironies, distilling them into a cauldron of quite merciless clarity. There is a morass of emotion, here – passive aggression, challenge, defiance, feminism, resignation and regret.

She deals in contrasts – droplets of ideas that are fermented into frequent antithesis.

When I was only fifteen,
I longed for you to hold me for hours.
Now you hold me for hours
and I long to be fifteen again.
—'(CU)RATING LIFE'

We used to spend hours talking:
Now we spend hours – in silence!

—'(UN)CONSCIOUSNESS'

If you appreciate the constructs of mathematics, astronomy and physics, there are allusions enough to satisfy. If you enjoy the whimsical, there is that, too – *if we were thinkers on some other planet and we ate breadsticks that finish the straight line of our lives* – mostly, though, there is a hard look at reality, dreams and their dissonance.

A poignant piecing together of simile, irony and hypothetical equation to create a thoroughly thought-provoking read.

—Hayley Ann Solomon, Author of *Celestial Promise* and writer of Prize-winning poems in successive annual competitions for the International Proverse Poetry Prize.
August 2021

Biljana Perchinkova

We receive the impression that Marta Markoska poured out this book of poems in one breath (given that every poem is packed with meaning, vividness and wholeness), but actually it is the result of a deeply mature search by an individual who seeks nothing more than the purest essence of its being. For in her poems Marta is *Ipsissima*, “the established authority”.

It is no coincidence that the title of this book borrows a term form astronomy, “black holes”. Marta’s verses are mathematically strict and cut like a knife. She asks us to cross

“nine hills
nine fields
nine seas”

(in the poem ‘Applied Geography’) so we can reach her shores.

Her poems have no gravity (‘No Gravity Poem’) and she circles “life like a free electron (in) constant orbit searching”. But, is the orbit really necessary to our wonderful poetess? For the orbit is round, and she is endless.

She writes to her companion, who is “filled with stories”, bringing him back from illusion to reality (as in ‘You Are Filled with Stories, And Here I Am Writing You Poems’). She is searching for the ‘Essence of Love’, refusing to measure her restlessness in pimples on the chin, her passion in the length of his sideburns, her love by the distance between his eyes, and her youth in the pills that keep us healthy. She will not allow her essence to be measured in electricity and heating bills. Because “the measure we use to measure” will be that by which “we’ll be measured” – and we are timeless.

Finally, the universe that Marta Markoska so selflessly shares with us is a counterbalance of reasoning that is indispensably limited (as in ‘Counterbalance of Reasoning’).

Astrophysics irreversibly confirms that the ratio between the total mass of the host galaxy and the mass of the supermassive black hole at its centre is a constant, regardless of whether the galaxy is active and vigorously shines with the quasar of its core, or not.

Consequently, the supermassive black hole forever remains the creative force that made the galaxy, and not a destructive swallower of the space-time entity. This is even more true for "Black Holes Within Us"!

Marta Markoska's poems are fist-tight zen koans; they are a hot sweet chestnut in the mouth that we can neither swallow, nor spit out, until the vivid pulsating reality irrevocably bursts in front of us. Like omniexistence, she desires to know herself. She is a "star that crumpled in its own gravity" ('Quantum Theory of Love') and now returns disembodied in the space-time entity. Marta multiplies her poetic (in)equations by zero, just as the quantum physicist genius, Richard Feynman, did before her, resulting in an electron that comes back from the future instead of a positron that travels from the past.

For Marta, it doesn't matter if we go up or down ('Counterbalance of Reasoning') and she wishes Newton was born in the same era with Heisenberg. We can only asume how the master of absolute space and absolute time (Newton) would face the Uncertainty Principle of modern physics. The only mathematical cross-section of this encounter would be (presumably) absolute silence, similar to what she says in '(Un) Counsciousness':

"We used to spend hours talking
Now we spend hours – in silence!"

This is where I finish my brief attempt to shine a light on what Marta has written, because this award-winning book of poetry, *Black Holes Within Us*, by the poetess (scholar and philosopher) Marta Markoska, does not tolerate long, mechanical and methodologically deliberate analyses. It is to be experienced.

—Biljana Perchinkova

Ivan Dzeparoski

In this era of Verlust der Mitte, as pointed out in the mid-twentieth century by the Austrian historian and art theoretician Hans Sedlmeier, in this age where the modern world is progressively losing its stability and solidity, as it shifts its state of aggregation and becomes a Liquid Modern World – in the words of the famous contemporary sociologist and culture theoretician Siegfried Bauman, and art even shifts into l'état gazeux, as pointed out by the French philosopher and aesthete Yves Michaud, in this world which many people also entitle a postmodern world, it is truly difficult to think and to write about "the black holes within us" created by that very world!

Furthermore, if these "black holes within us" are a harvest of the contradictory plausible-implausible desire for love, in these times where love is addressed as something that "has come and gone", as something "romantic" which needs to be analyzed and deconstructed, as something which only exists in the old books or in the new tear-jerking movies and soap operas, then the attempt to write poems about the "back holes within us", harvested from the realized-unrealized or plausible-implausible love, is a truly difficult and responsible feat.

On the other hand, the famous Italian philosopher, semiologist and prose writer Umberto Eco believed that "the postmodern reply to the modern consists of recognizing that the past, since it cannot really be destroyed, because its destruction leads to silence, must be revisited: but with irony, not innocently."

It is precisely with irony that Marta Markoska "brings back" time, revealing "the black holes within us", which, just as in the poem '(Un)Consciousness', lead to the following poetic-ironic and personally self-ironic notions:

"We used to spend hours talking
Now we spend hours – in silence!"

It is why the wording in “Areas of Love”, from the eponymous cycle in the book, is filled with expectedly-unexpected displays of states which ironically lead to poems with significant titles: ‘You are full of stories, and here I am writing you poems!’, or ‘Essence of Love’, or ‘Logic of the Stronger One’ followed by ‘Logic of the Weaker One’!

The poetry in the cycle “Applied Knowledge” can be understood in the spirit of a fervent and profound reader, and with the related title in a Frommian style, such as “Applied Crafts / Masteries / Arts of Love”, and with that, in the context of postmodern colloquial irony, we poetically discover how the applied sciences of history, geography, biology, chemistry, mathematics, physics, astronomy, sociology, economy and so on, lead us to “applied relativity” and Heisenberg’s “uncertainty” principle, and with that also to the “holograms of happiness” as possible holograms of love!

It is, therefore, no coincidence that the final cycle bears the title of the book, “Black holes within us”. After all, astronomers and physicists should be left to deal with the scientific interpretation of black holes, but when poets and poetesses transfer those “black holes” within “us”, those black holes find a “poetic home” in us, and find their poetic “refuge in method”. Even when this refuge is nothing but a post-festum notion for the ‘Enthropy of Love’, expressed in the lines:

“I once was making chaos in your system
not to prove to you the existence of the entropy
generated whenever our two bodies
were in a ratio to one another
(...)
I now assure you that two formations, two bodies, two
souls create much greater entropy
than any individual body for itself!”

The salty-sweet poetic pieces which Markoska serves us, giving insight into her own poetic image of the salty-sweet universe of love, is more than a successful poetic guide through her own galaxy of poetry. This book of poetry is also a subtle poetic plunge into the "black holes within us", which every honest reader finds not only in Markoska's poetry, but also deep within themselves.

—Ivan Dzeparoski

BIOGRAPHY OF MARTA MARKOSKA

Marta Markoska (b. 29 June, 1981, Skopje) graduated from the Depament of Comparative Literature at the Faculty of Philology "Blaze Koneski" in Skopje, and earned her MA at the Cultural Studies at the Institute of Macedonian Literature in Skopje. She is the first recipient of the "Todor Chalovski" prize awarded to a young Macedonia writer to recognize exceptional promise and contribution in the fields of poetry, literary criticism, essays and creative writing. The award resulted in publication of the bi-lingual (Macedonian-English) edition of the book "Black Holes Within Us" by GALIKUL - Association for culture, literature and art from Skopje founded in 2007 by Todor Chalovski (1945-2015), one of the most eminent Macedonian writers. To this date, Markoska has published thirteen publications. Besides the above-mentioned book, she is also author of the monolingual English-language H/ERO/T/IC BOOK (sensual – erotic poetry, Published in Hong Kong, by Proverse Publishing House, 2020), the bilingual Macedonian-English H/ERO/T/IC BOOK (First Edition, published in Skopje, 2019), FIL/L/M/ED STOR/I/ES (Scientific studies and Essays for Film and Cinematography, Eurobalkan Institute, Skopje, 2017), the Macedonian-English bilingual "BLACK HOLES WITHIN US" (poetry, first edition, House of Culture "Koco Racin"- Skopje, 2014), "CULTURE AND MEMORY" (cultural studies, "Matica makedonska", Skopje, 2014), "DISCUSSION ABOUT ZEN BUDDHISM: Religious and Philosophical Transcendence Between Eastern and Western Thought" (scientific study, "Matica makedonska", Skopje, 2013), "HEADFIRST TOWARDS THE HEIGHTS" (poetry, second edition, "Magor", Skopje, 2013), "HEADFIRST TOWARD THE HEIGHTS" (poetry, first edition, OU Centre for Culture "Aco Karamanov", Radovish, 2012), "HYPER HYPOTHESES" (essays, Institute of Macedonian Literature, Skopje, 2011), "WHIRLPOOL IN BETHLEHEM" (stories, "Templum",

Skopje, 2010) and "ALL TRIBUTARIES FLOW INTO MY BASIN" (poetry, "Templum", Skopje, 2009). Markoska is a recipient of the following awards: "Aco Karamanov" (2012), for the poetic manuscript "Headfirst Toward The Heights" and "Beli Mugri" (2014), for the poetry manuscript "Black Holes Within Us." Also, she is awarded in a short story competition "Nova Makedonija" (2015) for the story "Heights of Felix" and was a first place winner of the short story competition "Elektrolit" (2007) for the story "What happens when you're reading Frazer". Her work is included in several anthologies of contemporary poetry and prose. She is a member of the Writers' Association of Macedonia since 2012.

Markoska's biggest ideological project is The Humanitarian and Motivational Campaign, LARGER THAN LIFE – Beauty and Health of a Woman After Breast Cancer on which she is a creator and a role-model and a motivational speaker.

SOME POETRY AND POETRY COLLECTIONS
Published by Proverse Hong Kong

Alphabet, by Andrew S. Guthrie. 2015.

Astra and Sebastian, by L.W. Illsley. 2011.

Bliss of Bewilderment, by Birgit Bunzel Linder. 2017.

The Burning Lake, by Jonathan Locke Hart. 2016.

Celestial Promise, by Hayley Ann Solomon. 2017.

Chasing light, by Patricia Glinton Meicholas. 2013.

China suite and other poems,
by Gillian Bickley. 2009.

Epochal Reckonings, by J.P. Linstroth, 2020.

For the record and other poems of Hong Kong,
by Gillian Bickley. 2003.

Frida Kahlo's cry and other poems,
by Laura Solomon. 2015.

Grandfather's Robin, by Gillian Bickley, 2020.

Heart to Heart: Poems, by Patty Ho. 2010.

H/ERO/T/IC BOOK by Marta Markoska 2020.

Home, away, elsewhere,
by Vaughan Rapatahana. 2011.

Hong Kong Growing Pains, by Jon Ng. 2020.

Immortelle and bhandaaraa poems,
by Lelawattee Manoo-Rahming. 2011.

In vitro, by Laura Solomon. 2nd ed. 2014.

Irreverent poems for pretentious people, by Henrik Hoeg. 2016.

The layers between (essays and poems), by Celia Claase. 2015.

Of leaves & ashes, by Patty Ho. 2016.

Life Lines, by Shahilla Shariff. 2011.

Mingled voices: the international Proverse Poetry Prize anthology 2016, edited by Gillian and Verner Bickley. 2017.

Mingled voices 2: the international Proverse Poetry Prize anthology 2017, edited by Gillian and Verner Bickley. 2018.

Mingled voices 3: the international Proverse Poetry Prize anthology 2018, edited by Gillian and Verner Bickley. 2019.

Mingled voices 4: the international Proverse Poetry Prize anthology 2019, edited by Gillian and Verner Bickley. 2020.

Mingled voices 5: the international Proverse Poetry Prize anthology 2020, edited by Gillian and Verner Bickley. 2021.

Mingled voices 6: the international Proverse Poetry Prize anthology 2021, edited by Gillian and Verner Bickley. 2022. *(Scheduled)*

Moving house and other poems from Hong Kong, by Gillian Bickley. 2005.

Over the Years: Selected Collected Poems, 1972-2015, by Gillian Bickley. 2017.

Painting the borrowed house: poems, by Kate Rogers. 2008.

Perceptions, by Gillian Bickley. 2012.

Poems from the Wilderness,
by Jack Mayer, 2020.

Rain on the pacific coast,
by Elbert Siu Ping Lee. 2013.

refrain, by Jason S. Polley. 2010.

Savage Charm, by Ahmed Elbeshlawy. 2019.

Shadow play, by James Norcliffe. 2012.

Shadows in deferment, by Birgit Bunzel Linder. 2013.

Shifting sands, by Deepa Vanjani. 2016.

Sightings: a collection of poetry, with an essay, 'communicating poems', by Gillian Bickley. 2007.

Smoked pearl: poems of Hong Kong and beyond,
by Akin Jeje (Akinsola Olufemi Jeje). 2010.

Of symbols misused, by Mary-Jane Newton. 2011.

The Hummingbird Sometimes Flies Backwards, by D.J. Hamilton. 2019.

The Year of the Apparitions, by José Manuel Sevilla. 2020.

Unlocking, by Mary-Jane Newton. March 2014.

Violet, by Carolina Ilica. March 2019.

Wonder, lust & itchy feet, by Sally Dellow. 2011.

FIND OUT MORE ABOUT PROVERSE AUTHORS, BOOKS, EVENTS AND LITERARY PRIZES

Visit our website: http://www.proversepublishing.com
Visit our distributor's website: www.cup.cuhk.edu.hk
Follow us on Twitter: twitter.com/Proversebooks
"Like" us on www.facebook.com/ProversePress

Request our free E-Newsletter
Send your request to info@proversepublishing.com.

Availability
Available in Hong Kong and world-wide from our Hong Kong based distributor, the Chinese University of Hong Kong Press, The Chinese University of Hong Kong, Shatin, NT, Hong Kong SAR, China.
See the Proverse page on their website: https://cup.cuhk.edu.hk/Proversehk

All titles are available from Proverse Hong Kong, http://www.proversepublishing.com

Most titles can be ordered online from amazon (various countries).

Stock-holding retailers
Hong Kong (CUHKP, Bookazine)
Canada (Elizabeth Campbell Books),
Andorra (Llibreria La Puça, La Llibreria).

Orders may be made from bookshops
in the UK and elsewhere.

Ebooks
Most of our titles are available also as Ebooks.

www.ingramcontent.com/pod-product-compliance
Ingram Content Group UK Ltd.
Pitfield, Milton Keynes, MK11 3LW, UK
UKHW022006190726
13853UKWH00004B/1777

9 789888 492329